HOW I CHANGED the WORLD

Nikola Tesla

WORLD BOOK

Nikola Tesla

WORLD
BOOK

CONTENTS

World Book, Inc.
180 North LaSalle Street
Suite 900
Chicago, Illinois 60601
USA

For information about other "How I Changed the World" titles, as well as other World Book print and digital publications, please go to **www.worldbook.com**.

For information about other World Book publications, call 1-800-WORLDBK (967-5325).

For information about sales to schools and libraries, call 1-800-975-3250 (United States) or 1-800-837-5365 (Canada).

Library of Congress Cataloging-in-Publication Data for this volume has been applied for.

How I Changed the World
ISBN: 978-0-7166-2278-9 (set, hc.)

Nikola Tesla
ISBN: 978-0-7166-2284-0 (hc.)

Also available as:
ISBN: 978-0-7166-2290-1 (e-book)

Printed in China by Shenzhen Wing King Tong Paper Products Co., Ltd., Shenzhen, Guangdong
1st printing July 2018

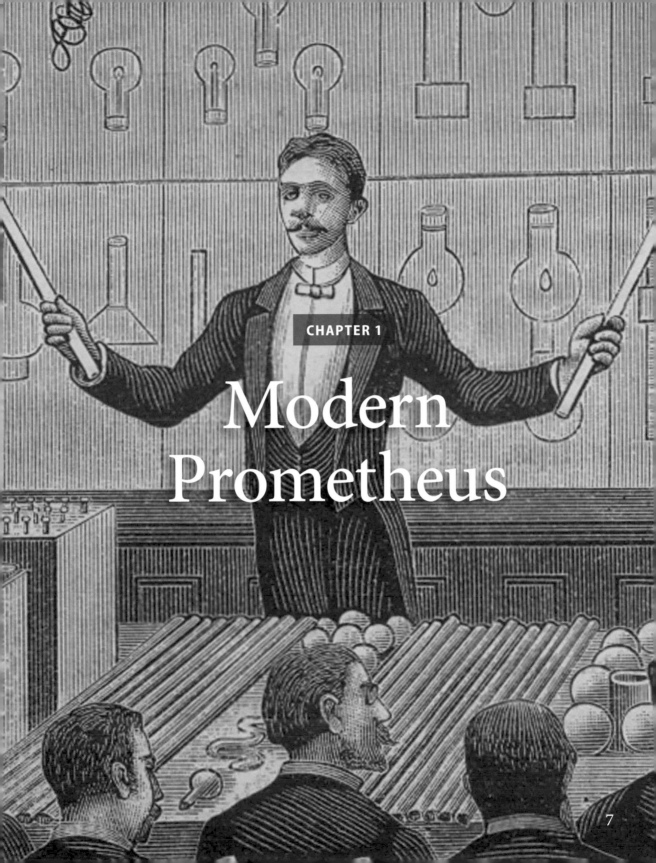

CHAPTER 1

Modern Prometheus

Early Years

Nikola Tesla (1856-1943) was a Serbian American inventor, engineer, and physicist known for his contributions to the modern alternating current (AC) system of electric power used around the world today. Alternating current is electric current that changes direction many times a second. Alternating current is easier for electric power plants to produce than direct current. It is also easier to increase the voltage of alternating current so it retains more energy as it travels through power lines. Nikola also developed several inventions that helped make wireless communication possible. Wireless communication involves sending and receiving information through the air or space rather than wires or cables. Nikola's handiwork can be seen in everything from the remote control to guided-missile technology. (A guided missile is a flying missile that is steered to its target from a site far away.) Nikola once worked for the American inventor and businessman Thomas Alva Edison (1847-1931). Nikola eventually parted ways with Edison to become his competitor in the so-called "war of the currents." A true visionary, Nikola always remained focused on the next technological breakthrough. His ideas in the field of electricity helped to create billion-dollar companies in the United States. Unfortunately, however, Nikola failed to protect his work legally and commercially. As a result, he ended up penniless while others made their fortunes with his inventions.

Nikola's family lived in the village of Smiljan (*SMEEL yahn*), in the mountainous region of Lika. Now part of the Republic of Croatia in southeastern

Europe, Lika was then a province of the Austro-Hungarian Empire. Nikola's parents, Milutin Tesla and Djuka Mandic, were married in 1847. Milutin was part of a long line of Tesla men who had served in the military. However, he had no intention of continuing the proud tradition. He was an intellectual, writer, and poet, owning a large collection of books on a variety of topics. He spoke several languages and had a natural talent at mathematics. Milutin also held strong political beliefs and wanted his people, the Serbs, to gain their freedom from Austria-Hungary. With many career options to pursue, Milutin chose his path in life based on his religious devotion and became an Eastern Orthodox priest. (Eastern Orthodox churches are the major Christian churches in Greece, Russia, Eastern Europe, and the Middle East.

Nikola's family lived in this house (below left) in the village of Smiljan, in what was then the Austro-Hungarian Empire (now part of Croatia). His father, Milutin Tesla, was the priest at the Orthodox church next door (right).

These churches are separate from the Western Roman Catholic and Protestant churches.)

Djuka, on the other hand, never received a formal education and remained illiterate her entire life. However, she and Milutin shared the same religious beliefs; her father was also an Orthodox priest. The spirituality they had in common made the two of them very close. Despite her lack of schooling, Djuka was well known for her incredible memory. She could recite several Serbian epic poems as well as long passages from the Bible from memory. Later in life, Nikola claimed his own photographic memory was one of the best things he inherited from his mother. Shortly after Milutin's *ordination* (admission) to the priesthood, the couple moved to Senj (*sehn*). Milutin was first assigned to a parish (church district) there and later to one in Smiljan. While Milutin kept busy with his pastoral work, Djuka was a dutiful housewife and served as the overseer of the small farm on which the Tesla family lived. She worked from dawn to dusk, but she was also an inventor in her own right. She devised sewing looms that greatly aided her in her work as well as churns and other labor-saving devices for the kitchen.

Nikola Tesla was born on July 9 or 10, 1856, amid the lightning and thunder of a rainstorm. He was the fourth of Milutin and Djuka's five children. His oldest sibling and only brother, Dane, was born in 1848. His two older sisters, Angelina and Milka, were born in

> *Nikola claimed his own photographic memory was one of the best things he inherited from his mother.*

1850 and 1852, respectively, and his younger sister, Marica, was born two years after him in 1858. Nikola was closest to his mother. Besides her knack for invention and a good memory, she also taught him a strong work ethic that benefitted him later in life. Nikola spent much of his early life working on the family farm. He was responsible for feeding the chickens, geese, sheep, and horses. There was also a large family of cats living on the farm. His favorite cat was named Macak. Young Nikola loved the animals under his care and spent a lot of time talking to them. This was Nikola's first interaction with the natural world around him.

One cold winter night, as Nikola stroked Macak's fur, he noticed the small sparks of light that were being produced on the cat's back. Seeking an explanation from his father, Nikola was told that it was merely *static electricity*, like he had seen during thunderstorms. Static electricity occurs when an object or material accumulates an overall electric charge. The charge can be released in the form of a visible spark. Nikola was fascinated by his father's response. He reasoned that this electricity must be some sort of power or energy. Instantly, he thought there had to be a way to produce more and wondered how that might be possible. Looking back on this event many years later, Nikola remembered thinking that if he could somehow find a way to put this electricity into use, he would be able to

Milutin Tesla, Nikola's father, came from a long line of Tesla men who had served in the military. However, Milutin (below) chose not to continue the proud tradition and became a priest.

power the machinery used on his family's farm. This was the beginning of his lifelong study of cause and effect.

Nikola's fascination with translating the forces of nature into usable energy soon took another step. He placed his toy boat in the small stream on his family's farm and watched as the flowing waters carried it away. Again, he imagined there were ways to use or control the power of the water's current. He experimented with small wheels and disks to do just that. Years later, Nikola traced his *patent* of a smooth-disk *turbine* (engine) to this experimentation. (A patent is a government-issued document granting an inventor exclusive rights to an invention.) Unfortunately, other concepts Nikola had as a young boy did not end with as much success. At one point, the idea of creating a flying machine took hold of his young mind. However, his exploration of its possibilities came to a sudden end after he jumped off the roof of the barn while holding an umbrella in his hand. After spending many months recuperating in bed, Nikola's parents ordered him to abandon this area of "research" and move on to other things.

For the most part, Nikola enjoyed a happy childhood, but a tragic event occurred in 1861 when he was just 5 years old. One day, his brother Dane went for a ride on his favorite horse. As Nikola watched, Dane was thrown off the horse and landed hard on the ground. Sadly, the injuries Dane received that day led

> *He reasoned that this electricity must be some sort of power or energy.*

to his death at the age of 12. Nikola was devastated by his brother's death. The terrible accident tormented him for the rest of his life, becoming a source of anxiety and stress. Nikola's parents were overcome with grief at the loss of their firstborn, and family life was never quite the same after that. Before long, Milutin requested a transfer to another parish. The memories of Dane's death were too closely tied to the farm on which they lived. Milutin thought that putting some physical distance between the family and the place where his son had died might help in the healing process.

Education

In time, his superiors in the Orthodox Church granted Milutin's request for a transfer, and the Tesla family moved to the nearby town of Gospić *(gaws PIHCH)*. This turned Nikola's world upside-down. He was leaving the only home he had ever known, along with all the farm animals he cared so much about. The change proved to be a difficult one for Nikola, but he got through it. His parents enrolled him in Gospić's primary school, and he quickly made new friends. In 1866, at the age of 10, Nikola began his studies at the Real Gymnasium (middle school) in Gospić. There, like his father, he displayed his natural talent at mathematics. His ability to solve complex mathematics problems in his head amazed his teachers. In fact, one of them was so astonished by his apparent skill that he accused Nikola of cheating before being convinced of Nikola's ability. However, Nikola did not excel in all his subjects. He performed poorly in his required drawing class. Years later, his inability to express himself artistically threatened to derail his career as an inventor. Even when it would have helped convey his ideas through diagrams, Nikola often refused to do so.

Overall, Nikola was a good student, despite daydreaming in class. In addition to his mathematics class, he enjoyed his studies of physics while at the Real Gymnasium. The various electrical and mechanical devices he found in the physics lab excited his curiosity. For the first time in his life, he had the opportunity to experiment with motors and water turbines. Nikola also read every book about electricity that he could get his hands on. His fascination with water power continued outside of school as well. At least in one instance, it had near-fatal consequences for him. One day, Nikola swam out to a nearby dam to study the water flow. Usually, the water rose to within a couple of inches of the top of the dam wall. That day, however, the water flowed swiftly over the top of the dam. Nikola did not realize how strong the current was. He was nearly swept over the edge. Fortunately, he caught himself at the last minute and slowly dragged himself to safety on the opposite side.

Nikola survived the incident with some minor bruising and a fever. He was forced to stay in bed, however, for the next several weeks. He used the time to read as much as he could, and he did not limit himself to books about science. He also read some of

His ability to solve complex mathematics problems in his head amazed his teachers.

the novels by the American humorist Mark Twain. When he met Twain many years later, Nikola told the author how his books had helped him through that difficult period, making him completely forget his "hopeless state." Twain was moved to tears by this encounter. The two men eventually became close friends. After recuperating from his illness, Nikola once again threw himself into his studies and completed his courses at the Real Gymnasium.

In 1870, Nikola went north to the city of Carlstadt (now known as Karlovac, Croatia) to begin high school. During his three-year stay in Carlstadt, he lived with his father's sister, Stanka, and her husband, Colonel Bankovic. Colonel Bankovic was a retired military officer of the Austro-Hungarian Empire who had fought in many battles. Nikola was happy to continue his scientific studies, but he found life with his new guardians to be difficult. Nikola's aunt and uncle did not feed him well and he suffered from malnourishment. On top of this, Nikola also contracted malaria shortly after arriving in Carlstadt. The city, located in a low-lying, marshy area where four rivers come together, experienced many epidemics of this disease. Nikola had to take a medicine called quinine throughout his high school years.

To escape the misery of his illness, Nikola focused on the study of electricity and mathematics. His

PHOT. BLANC
11. Rue de Buci.

HENRI DUPONT
Success?

As a student, Nikola's mathematical skills amazed his teachers, But his inability to express himself artistically threatened to derail his career as an inventor. Nikola is shown here as a young man in 1883.

favorite teacher was the physics professor. The professor often demonstrated scientific principles to his students with models, some of which he designed himself. One model was a large rotating bulb covered with tinfoil that would turn rapidly when connected to a machine that generated static electricity. Nikola was fascinated by his professor's demonstrations. "It is impossible for me to convey," he later said, "the intensity of feeling I experienced in witnessing his exhibitions of these mysterious phenomena. Every impression produced a thousand echoes in my mind."

Nikola was so dedicated to his studies that he completed them in three years instead of the usual four. He was eager to return home. He wanted to impress his father with everything that he had learned. Not only had he spent time mastering science, but Nikola also excelled in language studies. By the time he graduated from high school, he was fluent in at least seven languages: Serbian, German, Hungarian, French, Italian, English, and Latin. Milutin was

Nikola attended high school at Higher Real Gymnasium (right) in the city of Carlstadt (now known as Karlovac), Croatia. When he graduated a year early, he was fluent in seven languages.

indeed impressed with his son's newly acquired knowledge. However, when Nikola told his father that he intended to pursue a career in the field of physics and electrical engineering, Milutin was not happy. He wanted his son to follow in his footsteps and become a priest in the Orthodox Church.

When Nikola arrived back in Gospić, he found the city in the grip of *cholera,* a bacterial disease usually transmitted through contaminated water. Cholera can be fatal if left untreated. Milutin had sent word to his son, warning him of the epidemic. But Nikola ignored his father's warnings. Shortly after arriving in Gospić, Nikola fell ill yet again. He was forced to stay in bed for nine months. His condition became so bad that his family ordered a coffin in anticipation of his death. At Nikola's bedside, Milutin told him that he simply had to recover. With tears in his eyes, he told Nikola that he could not bear to lose

By the time he graduated from high school, he was fluent in at least seven languages.

another son. "Perhaps I may get well if you will let me study engineering," Nikola replied. Milutin had no choice but to agree to Nikola's wishes, and fortunately he recovered to pursue the career of his dreams.

Before Nikola could begin his higher education, an obstacle lay in his path. He had reached the age that required him to serve in the armed forces of the Austro-Hungarian Empire. However, Milutin was concerned that Nikola was not healthy enough to endure military training. Consequently, Milutin ordered his son to leave Gospić and hide in the mountains while he came up with a plan. Though avoiding service in the Austro-Hungarian army was a serious offense, Nikola spent nine months living in the mountains of Croatia with a hunter's rifle and a bundle of books. He was relieved when this difficult period ended, but he returned to Gospić stronger and healthier than he was before, just as his father had hoped. Meanwhile, Milutin had pulled some strings with his brother-in-law, Colonel Bankovic, to release Nikola from his military obligations.

In the autumn of 1875, Nikola began his studies at the Joanneum Polytechnic School in the Austrian city of Graz. The Joanneum (now Graz Technical University or *TU Graz*) was one of only four schools in Austria-Hungary that offered degrees in electrical engineering. Yet to make his father happy, Nikola enrolled in mathematics and physics with the intention of becoming a professor. He was now living more than 200 miles (322 kilometers) away from Gospić and his family. The distance allowed Nikola to finally have the independence that he had long desired. Once again, he outperformed in mathematics and physics. However, Nikola studied a wide range of subjects during his university years, including chemistry, botany, mineralogy, machinery construction, optics, French, and English. He also studied the writings of such brilliant men as the French philosopher, mathematician, and scientist René Descartes *(ruh NAY day KAHRT)* (1596-1650), the German writer Johann Wolfgang von Goethe *(YOH hahn VOHLF gahng fuhn GUR tuh)* (1749-1832), and the English playwright William Shakespeare (1564-1616).

Nikola's physics professor, Jacob Pöschl, took an early interest in his new student. "Pöschl was peculiar," Nikola recalled years later. It was said that Pöschl wore the same coat for 20 years, but what he lacked in personal charm he more than made up with his teaching. According to Nikola, "his demonstrations and experiments came off with clocklike precision." During his second year at the Joanneum, Nikola first formed the idea of creating an alternating-current (AC) motor as he listened to one of Pöschl's lectures. The school had recently acquired a *Gramme machine,* also known as a dynamo or magneto, from Paris. A Gramme machine was an electrical generator that produced *direct current* (DC). (Direct current is electric current that flows in only one direction.) By the end of the 1870's, Gramme machines were used to produce power on a widespread commercial scale. During his lecture, Pöschl used one of these machines

In 1875, Nikola enrolled at the Joanneum Polytechnic School (below) in the Austrian city of Graz, with plans of becoming a professor. The Joanneum is now Graz Technical University or TU Graz.

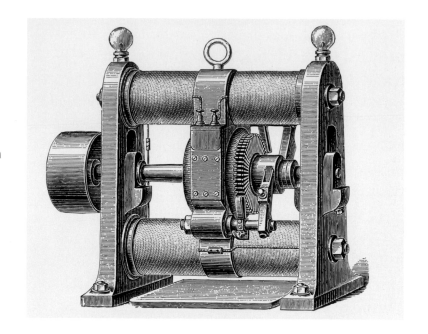

Nikola was fascinated by the new Gramme machine (right) at the Joanneum Polytechnic School. Nikola's physics teacher used one of these machines to teach his students about electricity.

to teach his students about electricity. Nikola was fascinated by the Gramme machine, but he noticed that it was inefficiently constructed and produced a lot of sparks. Nikola pointed this out to Pöschl during his lecture. There had to be a way, he said, for a similar machine to produce a more efficient alternating current. Pöschl thought that Nikola's idea for improving the device was impractical and immediately rejected it. Pöschl's stinging rebuke greatly embarrassed Nikola, but he remained convinced that he was right and his professor was wrong.

The disagreement with Pöschl was a turning point in Nikola's life. It forced him to broaden his view on the study of electricity. Gradually, Nikola began to understand that a motor was simply one part of a larger system. In time, he visualized a highly complex system that included a motor as well as a generator that delivered electricity to it to provide its source of power. Nikola would spend the next several years of his life working to turn his ideas about electricity into reality. Spending more and more time thinking through the details of his potential invention, Nikola neglected his studies at the Joanneum. He also began to smoke and became addicted to gambling. During his third year at the Joanneum, he gambled away all his funds, including his tuition money. In December 1878, Nikola dropped out of school.

Working for Thomas Edison

Not wanting to face his father's wrath, Nikola did not return home. Instead, he left Graz for the nearby city of Maribor in what today is the nation of Slovenia. There, he managed to find an engineering job, but he continued to gamble and lost a good deal of the money he made. In March 1879, Milutin learned that Nikola was in Maribor and went there to try to convince him to return to the Joanneum. When his son refused, Milutin suggested another school, Karl-Ferdinand University (now the University of Prague, also called Charles University) in Prague, and gave him some money to renew his studies. Nikola gambled that money away as well. When Milutin found out, he was very disappointed, but Djuka was more forgiving and encouraged her son to return to Gospić. Though it was difficult for him to do so, Nikola returned home and begged his parents' forgiveness.

Slowly, Nikola readjusted to life in Gospić. He was happy to be back in his father's good graces. Just over a year later, however, Milutin died, apparently of a stroke, at the age of 60. After his father's death, Nikola followed Milutin's wishes and resumed his studies at Karl-Ferdinand University. With the financial support of his two uncles, Petar and Pavle Mandic, Nikola had enough money to pay for his tuition. In January 1880, Nikola traveled to Prague (today the capital and largest city of the Czech Republic in central Europe). He arrived too late to register for the spring semester, but he signed up for summer classes and attended lectures on physics, mathematics, and philosophy. Nikola loved Prague. "The atmosphere of that old and interesting city was favorable to invention," he later said. During his time there, Nikola continued to think about his concept of an electric motor. Unfortunately, his uncles' money ran out, and he was forced to drop out of school yet again. In January 1881, he left Prague for Budapest (the capital and largest city of Hungary).

Nikola chose the Hungarian city for one reason. He had read an article in a Prague newspaper that the great American inventor Thomas Edison was interested in building a telephone exchange in Budapest. Nikola hoped to land a job there, but things did not work out quite as he had expected. When he arrived in Budapest, Nikola discovered that the company was not yet in business. He was forced to look for another job to support himself. Eventually, he found work as a draftsman in the Hungarian government's Central Telegraph Office. With his poor drawing ability, however, Nikola was not well suited to be a draftsman. Before long, he quit his job. His repeated lack of success caused Nikola to have a complete *nervous breakdown*. He was afraid he was going to die. (Nervous breakdown is a term once often used to refer to any-

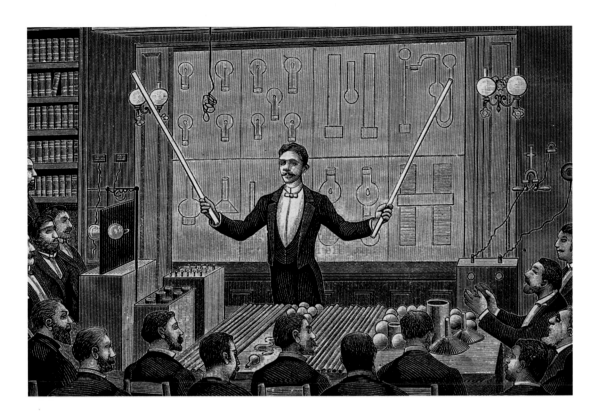

thing from fatigue caused by overwork to a severe mental illness.)

With the help of a former classmate named Anthony Szigeti (*SIHG ih tee*), Nikola slowly recovered. Szigeti was an engineer, and he and Nikola shared many things in common, including a love for the writings of Goethe. Going on long walks together in Budapest's parks, the two men became friends. Nikola also used these walks to discuss his concept for an improved electrical motor. Szigeti was impressed with his new friend's ideas, and he encouraged Nikola to pursue his goal. One afternoon, as he and Szigeti were strolling through the park, Nikola recited from memory a few lines from Goethe's famous play, *Faust*. As he spoke the inspirational words about the movement of the sun and

The above illustration shows Nikola delivering a lecture before the French Physical Society and The International Society of Electricians in Paris, France, in the 1880's.

invisible wings lifting the mind to new heights, Nikola was struck by a powerful series of images. In that instant, according to his 1919 autobiography, *My Inventions,* he came up with the idea of using a rotating magnetic field in his motor. "The images I saw were wonderfully sharp and clear," Nikola wrote, "and had the solidity of metal and stone."

Excited by his insight, Nikola wanted to show Szigeti what he had just conceived. Right there in the park, he grabbed a twig and diagrammed his invention in the soil on which he and Szigeti stood. "See my motor here," Nikola exclaimed to his friend. "Watch me reverse it." While his vision was incomplete, Nikola knew he was on to something. He knew what he drew that day would certainly prove that Professor Pöschl was wrong about alternating current and that he was right. Nikola knew this was another important

Thomas Edison installed a jumbo steam dynamo, also called a generator (below), to produce electricity at his first commercial power plant, Pearl Street Station, which he opened in New York City in 1882.

turning point in his life, since the path he needed to take—at least in his own mind—was now clearly defined. Even more important, he began to believe in himself. What he could not know at the time, however, was that his ideas would eventually change the course of the world. In time, he would be considered by many as a modern-day Prometheus (*proh MEE thee uhs*), the Greek god who stole fire from Mount Olympus and gave it to humanity. From this moment on, Nikola never strayed from the path of becoming a true inventor. Nevertheless, a more immediate concern demanded Nikola's attention. He still needed a job.

> *From this moment on, Nikola never strayed from the path of becoming a true inventor.*

Fortunately, soon after his life-changing walk in Budapest's park, Nikola found a job. In fact, the company that had brought him to Budapest in the first place, the Budapest Telephone Exchange, was now up and running. Nikola started working there at the end of 1881. Immediately, he impressed the company's owner, Ferenc Puskás, with his skills and abilities. Nikola made improvements to various installations, including superior amplification systems. Due to his outstanding work, Nikola quickly rose in the company's ranks until he was named chief electrician. His contributions helped make the Budapest Telephone Exchange a thriving business. It did so well, in fact, that Puskás ended up selling his company for a large profit.

When Puskás announced the sale of the Budapest Telephone Exchange, Nikola was concerned he might be out of a job again. Puskás, however, told him not to worry. He happily recommended both Nikola and his friend Szigeti to his brother, Tivadar, who was working on a new incandescent lighting system for the Continental Edison Company in Paris, France. Nikola was overcome with excitement. This was exactly the opportunity for which he had been waiting. In time, it might give him a chance to explain his ideas about an AC induction motor to Thomas Edison himself! When Tivadar Puskás heard about Nikola, he wasted no time in offering him a job. In 1882, Nikola moved to Paris with high hopes.

Before long, it dawned on Nikola that Edison's company was more interested in making a profit than anything else.

Nikola kept to a strict daily routine while working for the Continental Edison Company. He started his day before the sun rose and, no matter what the weather was like, he strolled down to the River Seine for a vigorous swim. He would then walk to the company's factory in the Paris suburb of Ivry-sur-Seine (*EE vree sur SEHN*). After a hard day's work, he enjoyed the many attractions of the French capital. He dined in some of its finest restaurants and played billiards with some of his new colleagues. However, his concept for an AC induction motor was never far from his thoughts. He was convinced it would solve many of the problems that Edison's company was facing in building an incandescent lighting system. Yet Nikola was often frustrated when he tried to explain his ideas to his co-workers. Most of them were not trained in physics or engineering and did not possess his understanding of mathematics. Before long, it dawned on Nikola that Edison's company was more interested in making a profit than anything else. This came as a deep disappointment.

Nevertheless, Nikola contributed as much as he could while working for Edison's company. He also learned a lot during this time. He came to understand how different types of motors and *dynamos* (machines that produce electricity) were physically assembled. It would be an important step in becoming a full-fledged inventor. Nikola spent a lot of time traveling as well. He went back and forth between Edison's companies in France and Germany, making necessary repairs to the equipment at various power plants. At one point, the company administrator of the Paris operation offered Nikola the chance to improve the operation of its dynamo electric machines. Nikola's solution for regulating the current produced by the dynamos so impressed his superiors that he was given greater and greater problems to solve. Several years later, he was also awarded a patent for the regulator he devised.

In 1883, Nikola went to Strasbourg, Germany, to solve the problems the Continental Edison Company was having with the lighting installation at the city's main railroad station. (Strasbourg now is within the borders of France.) His superiors thought that his knowledge, experience, and ability to speak German made him the ideal choice. Nikola worked night and day to fix the lighting system. In his spare time, he continued to work on his own invention. While in Strasbourg, he also constructed his first AC induction motor. Though the apparatus was crude, it was a huge leap forward. It was absolute proof that the idea he had conceived a year earlier did, in fact, work.

During his time in Strasbourg, Nikola became acquainted with several influential people with whom he shared his ideas about an AC induction motor. He asked them if they were interested in investing their money in his invention, but few seemed to grasp what he was talking about. This frustrated and disappointed Nikola. When he successfully finished his Strasbourg assignment, he thought he would at least be rewarded for his service to the Continental Edison Company upon his return to Paris. Unfortunately, more disappointment lay ahead for Nikola. Without receiving the payment that he thought he deserved, he abruptly quit. He was once again out of a job and did not know where to turn.

The Move to the United States

Just as his future began to look dim, Nikola received a helping hand from a man named Charles Batchelor. Batchelor was an administrator at the Continental Edison Company and also a friend of the great inventor himself. When Batchelor heard of Nikola's situation, he understood that Nikola's supervisors had not recognized his full potential. Batchelor thought that Nikola's skills would best serve Thomas Edison's organization by designing and manufacturing new and improved dynamos and motors. He wasted no time in offering Nikola another job. This one would not be in Europe, however. Batchelor had been called back to the United States to manage the Edison Machine Works in New York City, New York, and he wanted Nikola to come with him. Excited at the prospect, Nikola realized this was not an opportunity he could pass up. He quickly accepted Batchelor's generous offer.

In the spring of 1884, Nikola packed his meager belongings and sailed for the United States aboard the S.S. *Saturnia*. Among his most precious possessions were the poetry and articles he had written, his designs for a flying machine, and a letter of recommendation written by Batchelor to Thomas Edison himself. Nikola spent most of his time alone on the *Saturnia*, occupying himself with thoughts of his AC induction motor. The opportunity to work in the New World with a man like Thomas Edison filled him with great hope for the future. When he arrived in New York City in June, Nikola had only a few cents to his name. But he was certain his fortunes were about to change.

Before Nikola could accomplish great things in the United States, though, he had to adjust to his new environment. Upon arriving in New York, he experienced considerable *culture shock*. Culture shock is a feeling of disorientation brought about when people

In 1884, Nikola sailed to the United States for an opportunity to work with the great inventor Thomas Edison (shown here with an early version of his phonograph). Nikola and Edison shared a deep interest in the field of electricity.

suddenly find themselves in an unfamiliar place. Nikola was accustomed to the polite ways of the Old World and found some of the people in New York to be rude. Though he was fluent in English, he had difficulty understanding the American sense of humor as well. As with most people, it took him a while to learn.

Shortly after starting at the Edison Machine Works, the 28-year-old Nikola met his new employer, the legendary "Wizard of Menlo Park." Menlo Park was the name of the rural community in New Jersey where Thomas Edison's most important research laboratory was located. Edison was already a famous man, best known for inventing the phonograph in 1877 and the incandescent light bulb in 1879. Nikola was shaking with excitement as he handed over his letter of recommendation from Charles Batchelor, and Edison did his best to make Nikola feel like part of the team. The two men shared a deep interest in the field of electricity and what it could do for the world, but they were very different people. Besides being a brilliant inventor and clever innovator, Edison was also an uncompromising businessman. Through sly and calculating tactics, he had built a highly successful commercial empire. It consisted of Edison Machine Works and the Edison Electric Light Company. His organization supplied DC electricity to many factories, restaurants, and other establishments in New York City, but always with an eye on making a profit. Nikola, on the other hand, remained a visionary with little business sense. Nevertheless, he was certain there was much to learn under Edison's guidance.

CHAPTER 2

The War of Currents

The Break with Edison

One of the first projects Nikola was assigned after starting at the Edison Machine Works was the development of a new *arc lamp* for a street-lighting system. An arc lamp is a type of lamp in which an electric current produces light by jumping across a space in a circuit. At the time, arc lighting was the most prevalent way to light city streets, but it required high voltages and could not be used with Edison's low-voltage system. This meant that Edison was losing out on contracts for lighting the streets of New York. Nikola spent several weeks coming up with a new design, though for various reasons it was never put into production. Another project in which Nikola was involved was the S.S. *Oregon*, the first ocean liner with electric lighting. For some reason, the dynamos aboard the *Oregon* were unable to produce the necessary power, and Edison dispatched Nikola to make repairs. When he succeeded in doing so in record time, Edison was greatly impressed with his new assistant. "From that time on," Nikola later wrote in his autobiography, "I had full freedom in directing [my] work." He was certain that he had proved himself in his employer's eyes, and looked forward to a long and productive working relationship with Edison.

Nikola was given many challenging tasks while working for Thomas Edison. The great inventor always seemed to want new and better designs for his motors and dynamos. On one occasion, the manager of the Edison Machine Works reportedly told the company's workers they would be paid a $50,000 bonus for new and improved types of dynamos. In that day, a bonus of that size would have been so large that no one would take this offer seriously. Nikola, however, took his manager's words literally and set to work on his new designs. He labored seven days a week until he produced what Edison was looking for. When Nikola approached his employer about being paid for his work, Edison is said to have laughed and replied, "You don't understand our American humor." Without getting the recognition that he felt he deserved, Nikola quit after just six months with the Edison Machine Works. During that time, he was never given an opportunity to present his ideas about an AC induction motor with Edison. This parting of the ways would have lasting consequences for both men and their careers in the field of electricity.

Shortly after starting at the Edison Machine Works (below), Nikola met his famous employer, Thomas Edison himself.

After his frustrating experience of working for Edison's company, Nikola was more determined than

ever to make his own mark. He began to organize all the notes he had taken about arc-lighting systems. He thought this would prove to be an important first step in promoting his concept of an AC induction motor. Yet Nikola, ever the visionary, failed to recognize the competitive nature of the up-and-coming industry of which he was a part. Up to this point in his career, he never gave a second thought about applying for design patents to protect his ideas. Thinking like a businessman was one lesson he did not learn from Thomas Edison. Unfortunately, it was a lesson he would have to learn the hard way.

Tesla Electric Light and Manufacturing

Shortly after leaving the Edison Machine Works, Nikola was approached by two New Jersey businessmen named Benjamin Vail and Robert Lane. The two men had read about Nikola's work with Edison in some of the technical trade journals and were excited by the innovation of electric lighting. They were eager to enter this new field and wanted to do business with Nikola. In December 1884, Vail and Lane hired Nikola and organized a company using his name. It was called Tesla Electric Light and Manufacturing. Nikola was made a partner and given shares of stock in the new company. Using the knowledge and skills he had gained while working for Edison, Nikola proposed that their company develop its own arc-lighting system. In March 1885, he met with Lemuel Serrell, Thomas Edison's own patent lawyer, and hired him to submit several patent applications to the U.S. Patent Office. The applications included a patent for a new type of arc lamp, a DC generator to power the lamp, and a regulator to control the flow of electricity. These were the first of more than 300 patents that Nikola would apply for during his career. At the same time, he tried to convince Vail and Lane to invest in his AC induction motor, but the two men made it clear they were only interested in an arc-lighting system.

By 1886, the arc-lighting system that Nikola had designed was being used in Rahway, New Jersey, to light some of the city's streets and factories. In August of that year, the New York trade journal *Electrical Review* featured a front-page article about Tesla Electric Light and Manufacturing. Nikola was thrilled to have such favorable attention in the press. Soon afterward, the patents for which he had applied were awarded by the Patent Office. Nikola immediately signed them over to the company in return for more shares of stock. Once this was accomplished, his relationship with Vail and Lane underwent a sudden change. The two businessmen were interested only in making a profit and no longer had any need for Nikola. They abandoned him and disbanded the firm they had named after him. In its place, they created a new company that reaped the rewards of Nikola's hard work.

Thinking like a businessman was one lesson he did not learn from Thomas Edison.

Nikola felt betrayed by Vail and Lane, but even worse, he could no longer use the inventions he had made. All he had to show for his time at Tesla Electric Light and Manufacturing was a stock certificate of questionable value. He did his best to put the upset-

In 1886, Nikola received a patent (right) for a new type of electric arc lamp from the U.S. Patent Office. It was the first of more than 300 patents Nikola would apply for during his career.

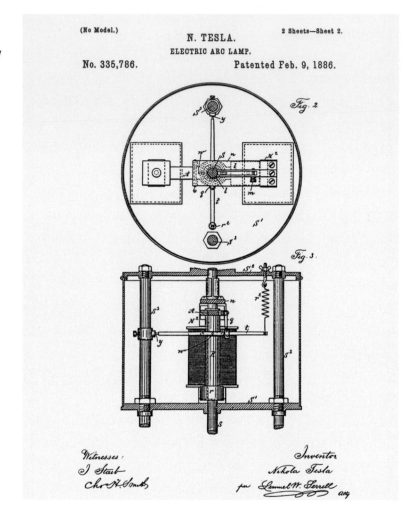

ting experience behind him and began to look for other work as an engineer or inventor. Unfortunately, he had no immediate luck and was forced to take a job digging ditches. Now 30 years old, an age when most young men in America had established themselves in their chosen career, Nikola found himself with a shovel in his hands. "My high education in various branches of science, mechanics, and literature [became] a mockery," he later said. "I lived through a year of terrible heartaches and bitter tears."

Despite his setbacks, Nikola was determined to make a name for himself. He knew that one way to do this would be to file a patent in his own name. He got an idea after recalling a dramatic experiment that had taken place at the Edison Machine Works in 1884. At the time, Edison was working with heated coal to produce an electric current, but the gas that was produced proved unstable and exploded, blowing out the laboratory's windows. However, this led Nikola to think about the relationship between heat and magnetism. He soon focused on the fact that iron magnets lose their strength when heated. By the end of 1886, Nikola had filed a patent for a thermomagnetic motor. In the patent, he outlined the basic principles of how the motor worked, along with seven different variations. This success paved the way for more and literally helped Nikola to climb out of the ditch in which he found himself.

Alternating Current and the Induction Motor

As he spoke with his fellow ditch diggers about his latest invention, Nikola was overheard by his foreman. His foreman, in turn, introduced Nikola to a man named Alfred Brown. Brown had joined the telegraph service about 10 years earlier and in time became the superintendent of Western Union's New York Metropolitan District. He held patents on several types of arc lamps and knew the limitations of the existing DC system. He was immediately impressed with Nikola's thermomagnetic motor and thought his ideas could dramatically change the industry. All it would take, in

Brown's estimation, was a little business expertise to turn Nikola's invention into a commercial success.

Wasting no time, Brown contacted a friend of his named Charles Peck, a lawyer from Englewood, New Jersey. Peck was interested in the telegraph and other advances being made through the study of electricity. He was also familiar with the lawsuits that were being filed by the various telegraph offices that were spreading across the country. With their combined experience in technical innovation and the business side of the industry, Brown and Peck were well suited to help Nikola succeed with his inventions. They knew how to set up companies and promote new technology. Nikola thought the two men would be able to advance the development of his AC induction motor. Fortunately, this time Nikola chose his business partners well. Years later, he called Brown and Peck "the finest and noblest characters" he had ever met.

Nikola would have to prove his fundamental theory that combining alternating currents could, in fact, produce a rotating magnetic field.

In the autumn of 1886, Brown and Peck rented a laboratory in Lower Manhattan in New York City. There, Nikola would turn his inventions into practical devices. Nikola's partners proposed that he receive one-third of the profits of their joint venture, while Brown and Peck would share a third. The other third would be reinvested to develop more inventions. Brown and Peck also offered to pay Nikola the money required to obtain the necessary patents as well as $250 a month. In return, Nikola promised to develop several other inventions along with his AC induction motor. In April 1887, the three men formally established the Tesla Electric Company. The following month, Anthony Szigeti came to New York City and began work as Nikola's assistant.

One of the first projects that Nikola worked on was his pyromagnetic generator. If successful, this generator would convert heat from burning coal directly into electricity. Brown and Peck were excited about this idea. Aware of the growing demand for inexpensive power in American industry, they thought this invention would be a tremendous breakthrough. Nikola labored on this generator until the late summer of 1887, but he was never able to perfect it, and the patent he applied for was rejected. At first, Nikola was afraid that his business partners would abandon him, just as Vail and Lane had done. However, Brown and Peck assured Nikola that they were confident in his abilities as an inventor. They encouraged him to keep trying. Following his partners' advice, Nikola returned his attention to the visionary idea he had five years earlier in Budapest: an electric motor with a rotating magnetic field.

Before he could reach this goal, Nikola would have to prove his fundamental theory that combining alternating currents could, in fact, produce a rotating magnetic field. He had spent a good deal of time thinking about this idea, but he had yet to put his ideas into practice. It was time, he knew, to go beyond the theoretical. Nikola's first step was to modify the Weston DC dynamo in his laboratory so that it could produce separate alternating currents. After much experimentation and using whatever materials he thought would work (including a tin can in which shoe polish was sold), Nikola achieved success. His generator delivered two separate currents to coils on opposite sides of his ring-shaped device, creating a magnetic field. Nikola was beside himself with joy as the tin can in the center of the ring started to rotate. He had done it!

Excited by his breakthrough, Nikola invited Brown, the more technically minded of his two patrons, to come to his laboratory for a demonstration. However, when Brown saw the tin can in Nikola's prototype (model) generator start to rotate, he failed to understand what his partner had accomplished. Brown wanted to know why he or Peck should invest their money in a spinning tin can. Nikola then explained how his rotating magnetic field could be used as the basis of an AC induction motor, which they could then sell on the market and make a handsome profit.

Even after Brown and Peck understood the potential of Nikola's invention, they remained skeptical—and for good reason. In America in the late 1800's, nearly all the electric power being used was direct current, not alternating current. However, Brown and Peck knew that the use of alternating current was beginning to expand in Europe. Before long, they were convinced that Nikola's invention had the potential to transform the industry. In May 1888, the Tesla Electric Company was awarded its patent from the government. Soon afterward, Brown and Peck reached out to a prominent physicist and engineer named William Anthony to see if he would agree to look at their company's new motor. Anthony happily agreed.

Brown and Peck then sent Nikola to Manchester, Connecticut, to meet with Anthony and demonstrate his new AC motor for him. Anthony was impressed with Nikola's invention. He mentioned Nikola's breakthrough during a lecture he gave to a gathering of engineers at the Massachusetts Institute of Technology (MIT) later that month. After hearing Anthony's positive evaluation of Nikola's new motor, Brown and Peck wasted no time in contacting the press. They had Nikola do demonstrations for Charles Price of the *Electrical Review* and Thomas Commerford Martin of *Electrical World*. Both men were likewise impressed, and Price featured an article about Nikola's motor. Brown and Peck knew it was just a matter of time before Nikola's invention received the attention it deserved.

One of Nikola's original AC induction motors, which he patented in 1888, is shown above. An improved version of the Tesla motor is the most widely used type of electric motor for power generation today.

George Westinghouse

As it turned out, George Westinghouse (1846-1914) was one of the first people who understood the potential of Nikola's work. Westinghouse, who was born in upstate New York, started his career in his father's machine shop in Schenectady. He created and patented his first invention, the rotary steam engine, at the age of 15. By the time he was 22, Westinghouse had invented air brakes for railroad cars and an improved signal system for the railroads. Besides being technically minded, he also possessed the necessary skills to run a business. In 1881, he founded the Union Switch and Signal Company.

It was not long before Westinghouse developed an interest in electric lighting, primarily to expand his business. In 1886, he founded the Westinghouse Electric Company. At first, he intended to use a DC system like the one Thomas Edison had developed. However, Westinghouse realized his company would stand to make more money if it had something different to offer. Also, Edison could sell his generators only to cities and towns with large populations because of their high cost. Westinghouse had to figure out a way to make a generator that served a greater number of people across a larger region. If he could, he knew he would beat Edison at his own game.

Westinghouse suspected that alternating current was the way to go. He was convinced that a large AC power plant built just outside any American city would generate electricity for the surrounding area efficiently and inexpensively. Once he decided on this course of action, he invested enormous amounts of time

Industrialist George Westinghouse (below) bought the patents to Nikola's AC induction motor and introduced the use of alternating current for the transmission of electric power to the world.

and money to make sure it was successful. By the end
of 1887, many American companies that worked in
the field of electricity were fascinated by the possibilities of alternating current. Yet this was not because
they thought it was the technology of the future.
There was still a large gap between the scientific
theory and the reality of the business world. Alternating current represented both tremendous commercial
opportunities as well as significant technical problems
yet to be solved.

For his part, Edison be-
lieved that alternating current
was simply "not worth the
attention of practical men." He
considered large AC power
plants too expensive to build.
Another concern was safety.

*...the press reported that the Tesla
Electric Company had produced a
functioning AC induction motor.*

Edison and his competitors were constantly seeking
better materials to insulate their low-voltage system.
Many of them did not think that Westinghouse would
be able to protect his customers from the dangers of
an AC system, specifically high-voltage electrical
shocks. However, the widespread doubts about alternating current came to an end when the press reported that the Tesla Electric Company had produced a
functioning AC induction motor.

When it was announced that Nikola was giving a
lecture to the American Institute of Electrical Engineers (AIEE), Westinghouse sent some of his most
trusted employees to hear what he had to say. The
lecture was a tremendous opportunity for Nikola.
William Anthony and Thomas Commerford Martin,

as vice president and former president of the AIEE, had made it possible. At first, however, Nikola did not want to give the lecture. He was ill and near exhaustion from having worked day and night on his invention for many months. Fortunately, Anthony and Martin convinced him to go through with it. Nikola's lecture, which he called "A New System of Alternate Current Motors and Transformers," took place on May 16, 1888.

As Nikola began his speech to the AIEE, he made a bold claim. He said that his new AC induction motor would soon be established as the superior way to deliver electric power in the world. Using step-by-step diagrams (which his partners had convinced him were necessary), Nikola then explained how his complicated *polyphase*—that is, multiple phase—system worked. The lecture was followed by a discussion. William Anthony praised Nikola's breakthrough design and spoke about how efficiently his motor operated. He also pointed out that the small motor that Nikola had brought with him was a prototype. The actual motor, when constructed on a proper scale, would prove even more efficient.

However, one of the men present that day was not so convinced of Nikola's achievement. Elihu Thompson, an engineer, inventor, and co-founder of the Thompson-Houston Electric Company, was critical of Nikola's design. Thompson also reminded Nikola that he was not the only one working on alternating current motors. There was a fierce competition going on, both in the U.S. Patent Office and in the marketplace. Aware of Thompson's reputation, Nikola politely stood

Nikola's AC induction motor (left) ranks among the greatest inventions of all time. It is widely used in industry and household appliances throughout the world.

his ground. He then invited his audience to come to his laboratory to see his motor in action. Over the next few days, all the major trade engineering journals and magazines covered Nikola's lecture and demonstration. Offers to buy his motor patents came rolling in.

Nikola entrusted the sale of his patents to Brown and Peck. He thought they would probably sell his invention to the Mather Electric Company, where William Anthony worked. His partners invited Anthony's company to make a bid on Nikola's patents, but they contacted several other firms as well. They reached out to Elihu Thompson, but he was not interested in buying patents from other inventors and declined the offer. It was then that George Westinghouse sent his company's vice-president, Henry Byllesby, and his chief corporate lawyer, Thomas Kerr, to speak with Peck. Byllesby and Kerr told Peck that the Westinghouse Electric Company was interested in Nikola's invention. They explained that Westinghouse's chief engineer, Oliver Shallenberger, had been experimenting with rotating magnetic fields for some time, but he had not been able to construct a practical AC induction motor. Peck then had Nikola demonstrate his motor for Westinghouse's men. When Byllesby and Kerr informed their employer that the motor's performance was satisfactory, Westinghouse told them to make a deal with the Tesla Electric Company.

The negotiations took several weeks, but the two parties agreed to terms on July 7, 1888. Brown and Peck sold Nikola's patents to Westinghouse for $20,000 in cash, $50,000 in stock, and $2.50 royalty per horsepower for each motor sold. The minimum royalty payment was set at $5,000 for the first year, $10,000 for the second year, and $15,000 for the third year. Brown and Peck were also compensated for all the money they had put into the development of Nikola's motor. In addition, Westinghouse paid Nikola $2,000 to come to Pittsburgh, Pennsylvania, for one year and serve as a consultant to the Westinghouse Electric Company. Nikola, in turn, gave Brown and Peck about half of the money they made from the deal with Westinghouse to express his thanks to the two men for all they had done for him. He kept the rest for himself. Bidding his former partners farewell, Nikola set off for Pittsburgh.

Market Competition

Nikola began his work in Pittsburgh in July 1888. During that time, he came to admire George Westinghouse. "Like a lion in a forest, he breathed deep and with delight the smoky air of his factories," Nikola later wrote. "An athlete in ordinary life, he was transformed into a giant when confronted with difficulties which seemed insurmountable. He enjoyed the struggle and never lost confidence." Nikola worked closely with Westinghouse and his engineers. Their focus was the development of motors that would serve Pittsburgh's power system. However, not all of Nikola's new colleagues were receptive to him. One of the main things they objected to was Nikola's proposal to run their motors at a frequency of 60 cycles (or 60 hertz) per second. Accustomed to running 133 cycles per second, Westinghouse's engineers resisted Nikola's ideas. It proved to be a difficult and frustrating time for him. In the end, Nikola convinced his colleagues to run Westinghouse's motors at a lower frequency, but he had lost valuable time arguing with them.

When Nikola's contract with Westinghouse expired in 1889, he left Pittsburgh and went back to New York City. Soon afterward, he was given an opportunity to travel to Europe. As a member of the AIEE's delegation, he attended the World's Fair in Paris. He marveled at the recently unveiled Eiffel Tower. He also learned about the intriguing experiments of the German physicist Heinrich Hertz, who had proved the existence of electromagnetic radiation and radio waves. Afterward, Nikola made his way to Austria-Hungary and spent some time with his family. While he was in Europe, the market competition in the field of electricity that Elihu Thompson had warned him about greatly intensified. The three biggest electric companies in the United States—Edison, Thompson-Houston, and Westinghouse—were doing everything in their power to corner the market. This rivalry, which had been slowly building for the past several years, came to be known as the "war of the currents."

The man most responsible for starting this "war" was Thomas Edison. He began a propaganda campaign that claimed Tesla's alternating current system was too dangerous to use because of the high voltage involved. Edison went to great lengths to protect his investment in DC technology by convincing the public that alternating current was unsafe to use. He found an ally in Harold Pitney Brown, an inventor from New York who wrote several articles attacking the use of alternating current. Brown was so dedicated to his cause that he was willing to commit cruel acts against defenseless animals to demonstrate the danger of Tesla's system. At one point, he offered 25 cents for every stray cat and dog that could be rounded up so he could wire them to an AC motor and electrocute them in a public display. When Nikola heard that Brown was torturing and killing animals to champion the cause of direct current, he was disgusted. Unfortunately, Brown's demonstrations convinced many people that alternating current was dangerous.

Thomas Edison explained away Brown's cruel acts against animals by claiming that it was done for a higher cause. Edison said he was interested in finding a more humane way to execute violent criminals. In 1881, a dentist from Buffalo, New York, named Alfred Southwick came up with the idea of the electric chair as an alternative to hanging. When Edison heard about Southwick's idea, he urged New York state legislators to adopt the electric chair as a means of capital punishment. Of course, Edison offered the services of his company to develop and perfect the device. At Edison's recommendation, Brown was appointed by the state of New York to oversee the

A competition in the field of electricity intensified between Nikola and his rival, Thomas Edison (left). Edison began a propaganda campaign against Nikola's new AC system, while going to great lengths to protect his own established DC system.

process of implementation. Brown immediately had a Westinghouse AC generator installed in Auburn State Prison. The first execution by means of the electric chair took place there on Aug. 6, 1890.

The man who was put to death was a convicted murderer named William Kemmler. His execution did not go well at all. After eight minutes and several failed attempts, however, Kemmler was pronounced dead. The following day, newspapers reported the event in gruesome detail. Edison did his best to blame the AC generator for Kemmler's cruel and unusual punishment. Years later, Nikola expressed his horror that the wonders of electricity had been used to extinguish a man's life. Though the Westinghouse Electric Company suffered from short-term bad press, the "war of the currents" ended with a financial merger. Its conclusion signaled victory for both alternating current and Nikola Tesla.

In 1890, Edison told Henry Villard, the president of Edison General Electric, that he had grown tired of the lighting business and was moving on to new ventures. Two years later, on April 15, 1892, Villard announced the merger of Edison's company with the Thompson-Houston Electric Company. The new corporation, called General Electric, owned patents in both AC and DC technology. As part of a patent-sharing agreement signed with General Electric, Westinghouse paid Nikola more than $200,000 for all his patents regarding alternating current. Nikola was now a wealthy man. For the first time in his life, he enjoyed the luxury of pursuing his own interests. He would soon turn his attention to new and greater challenges.

CHAPTER 3

Experimentation in New York

The Tesla Coil and Other Innovations

Upon his return from Europe in 1889, Nikola felt he needed a larger workplace where he could conduct his experiments. At the age of 33, he opened a new laboratory and began his research. He would work in a series of laboratories throughout Manhattan over the next several years. He also took up residence in the Astor House, one of New York's finest hotels. Though his fame was growing, Nikola remained a loner, with some noticeable eccentricities, one of which was an extreme fear of germs. He was often seen dining at Delmonico's, his favorite restaurant in New York City. He almost always ate alone. When necessary, he would meet with Thomas Commerford Martin, who had offered to become his publicist, or George Westinghouse's engineers, who would often question him about his invention as it applied to their work. Other than that, Nikola usually preferred his own company.

In search of a new field to explore, Nikola read up on the latest developments in electrical science and technology. He quickly became interested in three major areas: new methods of producing illumination, the delivery of power through wireless means, and the possibility of transmitting more information through wireless communication. These three goals would occupy all of Nikola's efforts for the rest of his life. As he began to study the incandescent light bulbs invented by Thomas Edison, Nikola was certain that he could produce a more efficient source of light. Only 5 percent of the power that was delivered to Edison's bulbs was effective; the rest was lost as heat. Nikola was inspired by Heinrich Hertz's experiments with electromagnetic waves that he had seen at the Paris World's Fair. He reasoned that the development of a device that worked at a higher frequency might bring about a technological breakthrough.

One of the central features of Hertz's machine was a large induction coil. However, Nikola was not satisfied with Hertz's design and came up with one of his own. He knew that to send electricity over a great distance would require a higher voltage. But if the voltage was too high, then his design would be too dangerous to use in homes and factories. After various experiments, Nikola was finally able to control the amount of electrical discharge as well as the frequency. On Feb. 4, 1891, he filed a patent for his new inven-

Several of Nikola's "Tesla coils" are shown below in a lab he operated in 1899. The Tesla coil helped pave the way for the invention of both radio and television.

tion, a machine he called an oscillating generator. In time, it became known as the Tesla coil. It was one of Nikola's greatest and most famous inventions, and it formed the basis of much of his later work with wireless power. In time, the Tesla coil would help pave the way for the invention of both the radio and television.

During his experiments with the Tesla coil, Nikola accidentally touched the end of a transformer and a high-frequency current passed through his body. Surprisingly, and to his great relief, nothing happened to him. This led him to discover that the current produced by the secondary coils had a high voltage but small *amperage*, that is, the strength of an electric current. Through this accident, Nikola also learned that the secondary coils would erupt in sparks if they were attuned to the same wavelength as the primary coil. When he attached the ends of the transformers to two spheres, the spark would jump from one to the other. The spark would then climb up the sides of the spheres, be extinguished at the top, and then start again at the closest point. (If this sounds familiar, it is. This apparatus, sometimes called a Jacob's Ladder, is often seen in movies about mad scientists like *Frankenstein,* the 1931 classic horror film.) Nikola also noticed that some glass tubes lying nearby were illuminated along with the spark. When he saw this, he knew he had made another important breakthrough. He had transmitted energy through wireless means.

> *…the Tesla coil would help pave the way for the invention of both the radio and television.*

The next step in Nikola's mind was to set up a dramatic demonstration of his discovery. During one all-night session, he sent his assistants out of the laboratory to get something to eat. When they returned, they found Nikola standing in the middle of the room with a long glass tube in each hand. "If my theory is correct," Nikola announced, "when the switch is thrown … these tubes will become swords of fire." He then ordered his assistants to turn out the lights and throw the switch. Instantly, the glass tubes in Nikola's hands began to glow and the light filled the room. Unaware of Nikola's wireless light theory, his assistants quickly became scared, thinking he was a magician or hypnotist of some sort. When Nikola saw the looks on their faces, he knew his demonstration had worked. He would soon capture the imagination of the public and attract new investors.

The year 1891 was momentous for Nikola. Besides inventing the Tesla coil, he also applied for several new patents. Among the most important patents were one for an electric incandescent lamp and one for an electric condenser. (A condenser is a device that receives and stores a charge of electricity.) He then asked Thomas Commerford Martin to organize a publicity tour to highlight his work with high-frequency alternating current. Nikola delivered another lecture to the AIEE at Columbia College, where he exhibited his "swords of fire" for his audience and left them in awe. Though some doubted his achievement, many more expressed their interest in his latest inventions. The emotional highpoint of Nikola's year, however, had nothing to do with science. On July 30, he became a naturalized citizen of the United States. At his swearing-in ceremony, he was filled with pride to call himself an American for the first time.

Seven years after arriving in his adopted home country, Nikola stood among the country's foremost inventors. With his growing fame, he received calls to deliver lectures in Europe. On Jan. 16, 1892, Nikola sailed to England aboard the *Umbria* and arrived there 10 days later. In London, he spoke to packed audiences that included Britain's leading electrical engineers and scientists. Nikola's demonstrations astounded both them and the London press. One reporter called him a "wizard who defied scientific explanation." Nikola then traveled to Paris, but his stay was cut short. After giving his first lecture there, he returned to his hotel and received a telegram that his mother, Djuka, was dying. Nikola immediately boarded a train and made his way to Gospić. The fear that he would not arrive in time to say goodbye was so great that it caused a patch of hair on his head to turn white overnight. On April 4, 1892, a few hours after her son's arrival, Djuka died. Brokenhearted, Nikola suffered another nervous breakdown.

One reporter called him a "wizard who defied scientific explanation."

The World's Columbian Exposition

Nikola spent the next several weeks recovering with the help of his family, who shared his grief at Djuka's passing. In May 1892, Nikola began a tour of his homeland. He went to Belgrade, the capital of Serbia, on June 1, and received a hero's welcome. King Alexander I bestowed on him the title of Grand Officer of Saint Sava for his extraordinary contribution to science, and the Serbian poet Jovan Jovanovic Zmaj read aloud a poem he had composed in Nikola's honor.

Nikola returned to the United States following his visit to Belgrade. With his mental and physical strength restored, he was ready for new challenges. When he arrived in New York on Aug. 27, 1892, Nikola established a new laboratory on the city's famed Fifth Avenue and later took up residence in the Hotel Gerlach (now called the Radio Wave Building). He also hired more assistants for his new laboratory. Before he set to work, however, he went on a brief lecture tour. In February 1893, he spoke at the Franklin Institute, the center of science education and research in Philadelphia, Pennsylvania. The following month, he addressed the National Electric Light Association at its annual meeting in St. Louis, Missouri.

Returning to New York, Nikola was eager to continue his work on his high-frequency inventions. At the same time, he wanted to improve his polyphase motors and hoped he could convince George Westinghouse to market them. Nikola was aware that the big European electric companies were moving forward with plans to develop a system for transmitting power with a multiphase current. Though he no longer had a contract with Westinghouse, Nikola did not want his invention to fall by the wayside in the United States. Westinghouse, however, had other priorities. His company was in danger of being forced out of business

Nikola's alternating current system illuminated the World's Columbian Exposition in Chicago (above) in 1893 in a spectacular display of lights for the whole world to see.

by the recently merged General Electric. General Electric controlled roughly three-quarters of the electrical business in the United States.

Facing a grim financial situation, Westinghouse knew he had to do something bold or his company would go under like so many other smaller electrical firms had. He quickly focused on the World's Columbian Exposition, the 1893 world's fair commemorating the 400th anniversary of Christopher Columbus's voyage to America. The Columbian Exposition was to be held in Chicago, and Westinghouse thought the exposition might be the opportunity his company desperately needed to stay afloat. If he could get the attention of new investors, he would then be more able to compete with General Electric.

The World's Columbian Exposition celebrated the many achievements of American industry and innovation. The fairgrounds in Chicago occupied 639 acres alongside Lake Michigan and consisted of more than 200 buildings. It was called the "White City" because the buildings were decorated with white plaster. Frederick Law Olmsted, one of America's foremost landscape architects, designed the layout. It took his workers three years to finish construction. More than 250,000 attractions were featured at the Columbian Exposition, including the world's first Ferris wheel. Another novelty was the widespread use of electrical power. Bids were solicited from America's electrical companies, large and small, to light the fairgrounds. More electric light bulbs were used there than in the rest of Chicago at that time! In the end, Westinghouse's bid of $399,000 won the contract. This meant that Nikola's AC polyphase system would be put on display for the whole world to see. Some have claimed that this was the last battle in the "war of the currents."

Winning the bid to light the World's Columbian Exposition was indeed a bold move for George Westinghouse. He knew that lighting the Chicago fairgrounds would be a severe test of Nikola's AC system. If anything went wrong, he would be ruined. Added to this stress was the threat of a lawsuit by Thomas Edison. Edison promised to bring swift legal action against Westinghouse if any of his patented light bulbs were used to light the fairgrounds. In response, Westinghouse came up with the "double-stopper" light bulb, which proved to be a much more efficient bulb than the one invented by Edison. In just a few months' time, the Westinghouse Electric Company produced thousands of these light bulbs for use at the exposition.

On May 1, 1893, United States President Grover Cleveland officially opened the World's Columbian Exposition. Standing on the balcony of the fairgrounds' administration building, Cleveland ceremoniously pushed a telegraph key made of gold and ivory. A moment later, thousands of incandescent lamps began to glow, illuminating the darkened fairgrounds. The crowd gathered in the White City gazed in awe at this electrical wonder. The Westinghouse engineers stood in Machinery Hall beside the 2,000-horsepower steam engine that made the spectacle possible. Nikola, who remained behind the scenes, had good reason to be proud. The polyphase AC system that he had designed for the Westinghouse Electrical Company had come through. At first, Nikola was not going to take part in the Columbian Exposition. However, George Westinghouse made a visit to Nikola's New York laboratory and convinced him of the need to demonstrate his system for the American public. Reluctantly, Nikola agreed.

The Electricity Building of the Columbian Exposition was scheduled to open in June. As Nikola traveled to Chicago that month, he began to realize that he had been given the opportunity about which he had long dreamed. When he arrived at the exposition, he went immediately to the Electricity Building and marveled at what he saw there. Inventors from all over displayed their latest electrical innovations. Thomas Edison presented his phonograph as well as an 8-foot- (2-meter-) tall incandescent light bulb that weighed a thousand pounds. Nikola was pleasantly surprised to see that the Westinghouse exhibit consisted primarily of his inventions.

On August 25, Nikola gave a lecture to a large crowd. During the lecture, he explained how the rotating magnetic field of his induction motor worked. Then he demonstrated the principles behind his invention. He began by asking the crowd if they had heard the story of the "Egg of Columbus." According to legend, he told them, Christopher Columbus convinced King Ferdinand and Queen Isabella of Spain to back his voyage to the New World by outsmarting the skeptics in the royal court. Columbus challenged his critics to balance an egg on its tip. When they

Nikola lit a large wireless light bulb (left) by allowing electrical currents to flow through his own body at the Chicago World's Fair in 1893. He was hailed as the "Wizard of Physics" following a series of dramatic AC demonstrations.

failed to achieve this feat, Columbus took the egg in his hand, lightly tapped the top of it on a table until there was a small crack in the shell, and then stood the egg on its tip. Impressed with this simple but clever trick, Isabella is said to have pawned Spain's crown jewels and financed Columbus's voyage to America. Nikola then announced that he could balance an egg without breaking the shell.

Like a master showman, Nikola produced a copper-plated egg and several brass balls. He then placed the egg on top of the wooden table beside him. When the egg stood upright, the crowd was completely amazed. Their astonishment only in-

Nikola invented fluorescent lighting. He is shown below in his New York City laboratory in 1898 lighting a wireless fluorescent light by conducting electricity through his body. An AC coil transformer is in the background.

creased when they saw the egg begin to spin. When Nikola placed the brass balls on the table, they began to spin as well. He quickly explained that a rotating-field magnet had been fastened beneath the tabletop. (He had used this same method years earlier to convince Brown and Peck to go into business with him.) Afterward, Nikola put on a show for his audience like the one he had given to his laboratory assistants. Those who saw the show would never forget it.

Creating an array of sparks with his Tesla coil, Nikola lit lamps of all shapes and sizes. For an exciting conclusion, he had a million volts of electricity pass through his own body. For a brief instant, Nikola himself became a source of illumination. Completely unharmed, he had disproven Thomas Edison's claim—once and for all—that alternating current was unsafe to use. Nikola's dramatic demonstration at the World's Columbian Exposition was the high point of his career, and it filled him with pride. By the end of the day, the press was hailing him as the "Wizard of Physics." For the moment at least, Nikola and his AC system had triumphed over his old rival, Edison. More important, he had helped to usher in the electrical age.

For an exciting conclusion, he had a million volts of electricity pass through his own body.

The Power of Niagara Falls

George Westinghouse's association with Nikola Tesla had saved his company from bankruptcy. After the World's Columbian Exposition, he was eager to build on his recent success. Years earlier, Westinghouse had heard about a project sponsored by the Cataract Construction Company to harness the tremendous power of Niagara Falls in upstate New York. Due to its location, Niagara Falls was an ideal place to develop a power plant to serve the needs of a large part of the country's population. In 1890, about 20 percent of all Americans lived within 400 miles (644 kilometers) of the falls. To oversee the ambitious project, the Cataract company hired a New York lawyer named William Rankine. Westinghouse was pleased to learn that Rankine had still not decided which electrical company to hire for the job. He was certain that Nikola's AC system stood a good chance of winning the bid.

Rankine knew that the Niagara Falls project would require an enormous amount of money and turned to John Pierpont (J. P.) Morgan (1837-1913) for help. Morgan was a wealthy financier and banker and one of the richest men in America. In the 1880's, when many railroad companies were in danger of going out of business, Morgan had stepped in to save them. However, he always demanded large amounts of stock and a seat on their board of directors. By the end of the 1890's, Morgan controlled most of the railroads in the eastern United States. He had also helped arrange the merger of General Electric. When Rankine told him about the project, Morgan was not excited about the idea. He refused to invest any of his money unless someone he knew and trusted could be brought in to supervise. Morgan proposed Edward Dean Adams. "If you can get him," Morgan told Rankine, "I'll join you." Adams was a Wall Street banker, a descendant of

U.S. presidents John Adams and John Quincy Adams, and Morgan's neighbor in New York City.

Once Edward Dean Adams was named the president of the Cataract Construction Company, he decided not to use the steam power generated by power plants in the small town of Niagara Falls, New York. Instead, he would utilize hydroelectric power plants in Buffalo, New York, and other nearby cities to supply energy for the construction of the Niagara power station. This would cut down on the project's expenses, but he would have to find a way to transmit the necessary amounts of power the 20 miles (32 kilometers) from Buffalo to Niagara Falls.

Adams immediately began looking for the best American engineers and scientists to determine the most efficient method to accomplish this. First, Adams consulted Thomas Edison, who naturally suggested the use of his DC system. Adams then went to George Westinghouse for his opinion. When Westinghouse learned of Adams's plan to use the power plants in Buffalo, he became concerned. He was still not sure if electric power would be able to compete with Buffalo's steam power in harnessing the raw strength of Niagara Falls. Although steam power was in wide use at the time, it was expensive to produce because it burned large amounts of coal or other fuels. Hydroelectric power, however, was still in its experimental stage. But Adams was certain that it would prove more practical and economical.

Next, Adams turned to engineers in Germany, Switzerland, and England. In June 1890, he brought together the industry's leading experts in the United

Nikola played an important behind-the-scenes role in helping to build this hydroelectric power station (above) at Niagra Falls, New York. The plant opened in 1895.

States and Europe and formed the International Niagara Commission. The commission then announced that a competition would be held to choose the best way to harness the power of Niagara Falls. Adams invited 28 engineering companies to submit a proposal. When Westinghouse found out about the contest, he was annoyed and refused to participate. "When they are ready to do business," he said, "we'll show them how to do it." The commission received a total of 14 proposals. Most of them were rejected for being impractical or too costly. This led Westinghouse to have second thoughts about the project. In December 1892, his company put in a last-minute bid.

In early 1893, Adams met with Nikola and asked for his opinion of the Niagara Falls project. Thinking the project would be a good way to advance his polyphase AC system, Nikola recommended it to Adams. He explained the problems that might arise with a DC system. After Nikola's performance at the World's Columbian Exposition, his name and reputation meant a lot to Adams. Based on Nikola's advice, the commission awarded a contract to the Westinghouse Electric Company for constructing a two-phase AC system at Niagara Falls. A second contract was awarded to General Electric to construct an AC power distribution system. The power plant built at Niagara Falls began transmitting power to Buffalo in 1896. Within the next 10 years, it was providing electricity across New York State.

When the American public heard that Nikola was working with the Westinghouse Electric Company on the Niagara Falls project, it was generally assumed that he was responsible for the monumental achievement. Nikola played an important, behind-the-scenes role in harnessing the power of Niagara Falls, but he did not design the new system that was put in place. Nevertheless, Nikola's reputation was greatly advanced by his association with the project. The success at Niagara Falls confirmed his standing as one of America's leading inventors and opened the door to new opportunities.

The Nikola Tesla Company

By 1894, Nikola's investigations of high frequencies had allowed him to create a new system of electric lighting and a steam-powered oscillator. (An oscillator is a device that converts direct current into alternating current of a particular frequency.) The time had come to promote his inventions and bring in revenue so that he could continue with his research. Fortunately, finding investors would be much easier after Nikola's appearance at the World's Columbian Exposition in Chicago. More than 25 million people had attended the exposition, and many of them had experienced there the wonders of electricity for the first time. Nikola's publicist, Thomas Commerford Martin, suggested that publishing a book would be an excellent way to attract attention. Nikola readily agreed.

Martin then collected all the lectures Nikola had given over the last 10 years, along with the many articles he had written, and began to organize them into a manuscript. The nearly 500-page manuscript described almost all of Nikola's inventions up to December 1893. The finished book, titled *The Inventions, Researches, and Writings of Nikola Tesla,* was published in January 1894. It proved to be quite popular, both in the United States and in Europe. The first edition sold out within the month, and a second edition was rushed to the printers. It, too, sold out by the end of the year. The book documented Nikola's work for future generations. It made a good amount of money for Nikola and succeeded in attracting the attention of new investors.

In 1895, Nikola decided the time had come to start his own company. He turned to Edward Dean Adams and invited him to visit his laboratory. After several impressive demonstrations, Adams agreed to promote Nikola's latest inventions. Together, the two men launched the Nikola Tesla Company. Eventually,

Adams invested over $100,000 (about $2.7 million today) of his own money. Since their joint venture would promote Nikola's recent patents as well as the ones assigned to Brown and Peck, Adams suggested they hire Alfred Brown as the new company's director. Adams also wanted William Rankine, from the Niagara Falls project, to serve on the board of directors.

The Nikola Tesla Company announced plans to manufacture generators, motors, and electrical machinery of all kinds. The company would also handle all of Nikola's patents for the next several decades. However, Adams did not consider himself an inventor. He was more of a promoter, and he likely saw the Nikola Tesla Company as an investment. Once Nikola's new lighting system and steam-powered oscillator were perfected, they could be sold or licensed to make a considerable profit. That was how Adams made a living as a Wall Street banker, and Nikola was aware of this. By attracting investors with Nikola's inventions, the Nikola Tesla Company stood to gain a lot of money.

Nikola invented many versions of his mechanical oscillator (generator) for producing electricity, including the small steam-powered oscillator pictured above.

Unfortunately, Nikola and Adams chose a bad time to go into business together. The United States was still in a deep *economic depression* after the Panic of 1893. (An economic depression is a severe reduction in business activity lasting for a long time.) Most electrical and utility companies made little, if any, profits in the years that immediately followed. Another issue was Nikola's lack of business sense. As always, he remained a visionary. New ideas for inventions were never in short supply with him, but converting these concepts into commercially successful products was another matter. Nikola always wanted to put off the difficult work of product development, that is, coming up with the best version of his inventions.

Nikola sits and reads in front of one of his inventions, a spiral coil of his high-frequency transformer.

This was apparent in the demonstrations that he gave at the time. Instead of focusing on the most promising design, he would present half a dozen variations. When Nikola developed his AC induction motor, he had relied heavily on Charles Peck's ability to market and ultimately sell it. Sadly, Peck had died in 1890. Adams and Rankine were clever businessmen, but they knew little about patent law or engineering. Consequently, Nikola was left without the proper guidance to make his company a success.

The Fire

On the morning of March 13, 1895, Nikola awoke to terrible news. The building on Fifth Avenue that housed his laboratory had been destroyed in a fire. The exact cause of the fire was never determined. It began in the basement and quickly spread to the upper floors. The following day, there was nothing left of the building but a smoldering shell. The fire was covered by all the major newspapers. "In a single night," the *New York Herald* reported, "the fruits of 10 years of toil and research were swept away." Charles Dana of the *New York Sun* referred to the destruction of Nikola's laboratory as "a misfortune to the whole world." All of Nikola's papers and notes (which he had recently brought to his laboratory to organize), along with several ongoing experiments, were lost. Though much of his equipment was housed elsewhere, his work on the development of wireless telegraphy and the wireless transmission of energy went up in flames. Wireless telegraphy, which later became known as radio, had seen rapid development over the past 14 years due to the pioneering work of Guglielmo Marconi and others.

Having invested around $100,000 dollars in his laboratory, Nikola suddenly found himself with no means of support. Worse still, he had not taken out a fire-insurance policy and did not have the funds to build a new workshop. He was devastated by his loss and went into a deep depression. For days after the fire, he left his hotel and hopelessly wandered the streets of New York City. Afraid for his well-being, Nikola's friends did what they could to help. Robert Underwood Johnson, an influential American diplomat and writer, and his wife, Katharine, offered to help him. Grateful for his friends' kindness, Nikola thanked them for their generosity. "I must carve my way through or over the mountain suddenly planted in front of me," he told the Johnsons.

Soon afterward, Nikola began to use electrotherapy, a medical treatment involving electrical currents, to help overcome his sense of despair. During his earliest experiments with high-frequency alternating current, he noticed how electricity affected the human body. Nikola was amazed how it seemed to change his mood. Recalling this, he gave himself electrical shocks on a regular basis over the next several months. He eventually came out of his depression, either through electrotherapy or the healing passage of time. In July 1895, Nikola opened a new laboratory on East Houston Street in Lower Manhattan, with the financial support of Edward Dean Adams and others. With a great sense of determination, Nikola was ready to expand his research into new and exciting areas.

CHAPTER 4

The Wireless Age

The Magnifying Transmitter

His new laboratory up and running, Nikola was eager to continue his experiments. While he focused on developing his ideas about the wireless transmission of energy, a recent discovery in the field of electromagnetic radiation also got his attention. In 1895, a German mechanical engineer and physicist named Wilhelm Roentgen *(REHNT guhn)* (1845-1923) produced and detected what are now known as X rays. The following year, the *New York Sun* reported that Roentgen had uncovered a "light that never was," which was able to detect things unseen by the human eye. For his groundbreaking work, Roentgen received the first Nobel Prize in Physics, in 1901.

When Edward Hewitt, the son of the mayor of New York, heard about Roentgen's discovery, he rushed to tell Nikola the news. A few months earlier, he had visited Nikola's Houston Street laboratory with Mark Twain. The two men had come by to see Nikola's latest experiments with photography that involved a device known as a *Crookes tube*. (A Crookes tube is a glass container that can carry electricity.) During their conversation, Hewitt suggested that Nikola take a photograph of Twain to mark the occasion. A few days later, Hewitt stopped by the laboratory to see how the picture had turned out. Nikola told him the experiment had failed because the light produced by the Crookes tube was too weak.

When Roentgen's discovery was announced in the newspapers, it was reported that he too had experimented with Crookes tubes. Hewitt, recalling Nikola's experiment with the same device, returned to the laboratory and asked to see the photographic plate Nikola had taken of Twain. What the two men saw there astounded them. The photograph had captured visible light as well as invisible radiation. In frustration, Nikola threw the plate to the floor, shattering it. If he had paid closer attention, *he* would have been credited with the discovery of X rays!

Nikola did his best to put this oversight behind him and spent the next few months repeating Roentgen's experiments. He called the X rays that he produced "shadowgraphs." However, it was not long before Nikola ended his research in this area. There were a couple of reasons behind his decision. First, he realized he would not be able to compete with the large companies that were already moving into the new field of *radiology*. (Radiology is the field of medicine that uses X rays and other means to create images of structures and processes inside the body.) More important, working with his shadowgraphs did nothing to advance his interest in the wireless transmission of energy. Instead, he focused on his ideas for remotely controlled devices.

In 1897, Nikola filed a patent for a radio-controlled boat. The following year, he revealed his invention to the public at the Electrical Exhibition held at Madison Square Garden. When Nikola made the boat move with his handheld transmitter box, the people there stared in disbelief. Many thought Nikola was em-

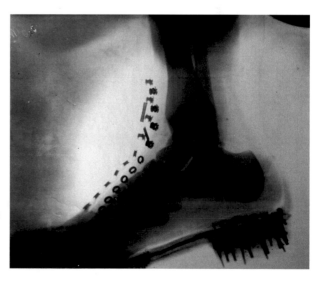

Nikola conducted early experiments with X rays, which he called "shadowgraphs," in 1894. He produced the X ray below of a human foot inside a shoe.

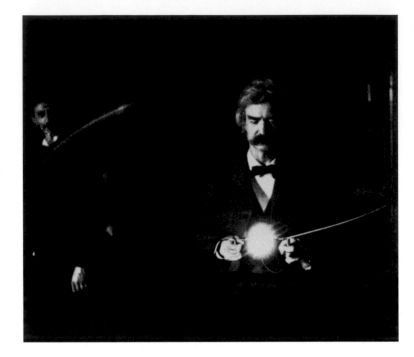

Nikola, standing in the background at left, conducts an experiment with Samuel Clemens (also known as Mark Twain) in this photograph (right). The photograph captured visible light as well as invisible radiation (X rays).

ploying magic or perhaps *telepathy* (mind reading). Some accused him of being a trickster and believed he had hidden a trained monkey somewhere on the boat. When the Spanish-American War broke out in April, Nikola attempted to sell his idea to the U.S. Navy. However, the government showed little interest, failing to see how his invention could be used in battle.

Around this time, Nikola began his association with John Jacob Astor IV (1864-1912). Astor's great-grandfather, for whom he was named, was the first multimillionaire in the United States. In the early 1800's, he made his fortune from the fur trade and investments in New York real estate. Astor IV met Nikola briefly when he was a director of the Cataract Construction Company, the firm that had built the power plant at Niagara Falls. Astor had followed his work closely ever since. In need of a new patron,

Nikola wrote Astor in January 1899. He asked Astor to invest $100,000 in the Nikola Tesla Company and become its majority shareholder. To Nikola's delight, Astor agreed.

Astor believed that Nikola was primarily interested in developing a wireless lighting system. Nikola, however, remained focused on his ideas about the wireless transmission of energy. At the time, it was impossible to transmit long-distance communication signals without the use of wires. By the late 1890's, Nikola became convinced it was possible to send electricity across great distances, either through the earth itself or through the atmosphere. With the promise of Astor's investment, he began looking for the best way to test his ideas on a grand scale. The opportunity Nikola was waiting for came when Leonard Curtis of the Colorado Springs Electric Company asked him to build a temporary power plant in his home state. Curtis told Nikola that he would provide him with all the land and electrical power he required. Jumping at the chance, Nikola moved to Colorado Springs, Colorado, in May 1899.

Colorado Springs, at 6,000 feet (1,829 meters) above sea level and with a dry climate, provided Nikola with the ideal atmospheric conditions to perform his experiments. The building where Nikola did his work was built just outside the city and had a beautiful view of Pikes Peak. He had a large wooden tower erected on the roof of this facility. The tower contained a retractable copper pole that rose from an enormous Tesla coil and was nearly 300 feet (91 meters) long when fully extended. Atop the pole was a copper ball that measured 3 feet (about 1 meter) in diameter. Nikola called this giant apparatus his "magnifying transmitter." With his magnifying transmitter, he conducted a series of experiments. In one of the most spectacular examples, he produced artificial lightning discharges that consisted of millions of volts and measured up to 135 feet (41 meters) in length.

One night while Nikola was hard at work in his laboratory, the magnifying transmitter received some mysterious signals. Immediately, he speculated that they had come from outer space. In the late 1800's, many Americans believed that intelligent life existed on the planet Mars. Excited by his discovery, Nikola alerted the press. Several newspapers reported that Earth had indeed been contacted by a Martian civilization. In 1901, *Collier's Weekly* published an article titled "Talking with the Planets." In it, Nikola suggested the signals had come from Mars, Venus, or some other planet. However, many people theorized the signals had come from experiments being conducted by Guglielmo Marconi (1874-1937), the Italian inventor known for his pioneering work in radio communication. Others have proposed that the signals were, in fact, extraterrestrial in origin, though not produced by intelligent life. In 1955, radio waves were first detected coming from Jupiter's moon Io as a series of pulses. Some scientists think this may have been what Nikola's magnifying transmitter picked up. Despite various hypotheses, the source of the signals remains a mystery.

In the autumn of 1899, Nikola prepared for another series of bold experiments. He wrote to his friend

Nikola's Houston Street laboratory in New York (left) shows two transformers and an induction motor. Tesla's research led to many important inventions.

Robert Underwood Johnson and asked him to write an article, complete with photographs of his magnifying transmitter in action, for *The Century Magazine.* Nikola decided it was time for the whole world to learn about his latest achievement. That December, the photographer Dickenson Alley arrived in Colorado Springs and captured one of the most famous images of Nikola through *double exposure,* that is, the repeated exposure of a photographic plate to light to create a single image. Nikola is shown sitting quietly in his laboratory next to the magnifying transmitter

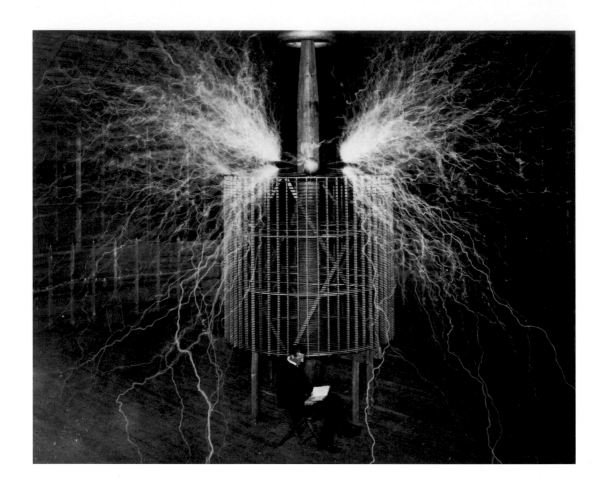

In 1899, photographer Dickenson Alley captured this dramatic image (above) of Nikola sitting next to his transmitter in his Colorado laboratory as a storm of electricity rages around him.

as a storm of electricity rages around him. Unfortunately, his time in Colorado Springs was unexpectedly cut short before the article could be published. During one of his last experiments there, Nikola accidentally short-circuited the electric company's main generator and caused a blackout in Colorado Springs and the surrounding area. This catastrophe led to Nikola's early departure.

Wardenclyffe Tower

Nikola left Colorado on Jan. 7, 1900. When he arrived in New York City, he was confident that electric power could be transmitted wirelessly across the world. In his mind, the next step was to turn his experiments in Colorado into a major invention. Returning to his laboratory on Houston Street, he began to prepare the necessary patents. He also began to look for new investors. John Jacob Astor, having lost interest in Nikola's work, failed to come through on his investment. Astor had told Nikola he would put up $100,000 for his wireless experiments. In the end, however, he gave him less than a third of the promised money. To drum up new interest, Nikola spoke to the press about his bold new plans. "My experiments have been most successful," he told one reporter. "I am now convinced that I shall be able to communicate by means of wireless telegraphy … with every city of the world."

When Nikola announced his plans to send wireless messages from America to Europe, many people simply did not believe him. One of them was his new chief rival, Guglielmo Marconi. Unable to send a wireless signal any farther than 86 miles (138 kilometers), the Italian inventor was not shy about expressing his doubts to the press about Nikola's plan. Ignoring Marconi, Nikola focused on funding his research. He turned to George Westinghouse but was unable to convince his old employer to invest any money in his new venture. But Westinghouse, out of his deep sense of loyalty to Nikola, loaned him several thousand dollars to get his new project started. One of the biggest problems that Nikola faced at this point was that he had left Colorado Springs without any practical invention that he could show to potential investors. Another issue was that he was simply ahead of

Nikola designed this early wireless communication facility (right), which was completed in 1902 on Long Island, New York. The structure was known as Wardenclyffe Tower, or Tesla Tower.

his time. The benefits of wireless communication were not immediately apparent to most investors at the beginning of the 1900's.

In June 1900, *The Century Magazine* published the article by Robert Underwood Johnson about Nikola's work. Titled "The Problem of Increasing Human Energy," the article was 70 pages in length and included several astonishing photographs taken in the Colorado Springs laboratory. In the article, Nikola explained his understanding of the role that energy and technology played in human history. He also talked about the elimination of war, the possibility of life on other planets, and many other provocative topics. Parts of the article were published in many newspapers and magazines in the United States and Europe. It made quite a stir and renewed interest in Nikola's research.

One of the influential people who was excited by Nikola's ideas was John Pierpont Morgan. Morgan, who had invested heavily in the Niagara Falls project, remembered the important part that Nikola had played. He was a mutual friend of the writer Robert Underwood Johnson and his wife, Katharine. Through the Johnsons, Nikola was given a chance to meet Morgan. Nikola spoke with him about the possibilities of wireless communication. He was certain his next invention would replace both the telegraph and the telephone. Morgan was fascinated. Over the next several months, Nikola wrote a series of letters to Morgan detailing his ideas. On March 4, 1901, the two men struck a deal. Morgan gave Nikola a check for $150,000 (about $4.1 million today) to

develop his invention. In return, he was given controlling interest in Nikola's lighting and wireless patent rights.

Once his deal with Morgan was concluded, Nikola began looking for a place to conduct his experiments with wireless communication. He decided to build a new facility on the Atlantic coast near New York City. Word of this quickly spread. During this time, Nikola met a man named James Warden, a banker and lawyer from Ohio. Warden had recently moved to Long Island, New York, hoping to make a fortune in real estate. He purchased 1,600 acres (about 648 hectares) of farmland near the town of Woodville Landing and named his property Wardenclyffe. At first, Warden thought it would make an ideal place for New Yorkers to spend their summer vacation. When he heard about Nikola's plans for a laboratory, he approached him with an offer to sell 200 acres (81 hectares) of land. In 1901, Nikola bought the property.

Nikola hired his friend and prominent American architect Stanford White (1853-1906), the designer of the Niagara Falls power plant, to draw up plans for his new laboratory. Construction began in September. The most prominent feature of the facility was the tower located about 350 feet (107 meters) from the laboratory. The tower itself was built by W. D. Crowe, an associate of White's from East Orange, New Jersey. It became known as Wardenclyffe Tower. The mushroom-shaped tower was 187 feet (57 meters) tall. It had a dome top that measured 68 feet (21 meters) in diameter and weighed 55 tons (about 50 metric tons). This elevated terminal was so large because of the vast amount of energy required to transmit power on the scale that Nikola had in mind. When construction was completed in September 1902, the press gathered to cover the event. Standing in the shadow of Wardenclyffe Tower, many reporters expected Nikola to send the first wireless message across the Atlantic. Unfortunately, they were left waiting.

From the start, Nikola's critics, including Marconi, doubted his claims about Wardenclyffe Tower. Marconi told the press that wireless communication was not yet possible, though privately he was working hard to achieve this same goal. Marconi's attacks in the press led many people to have doubts about Nikola and his latest project. Even Thomas Commerford Martin, Nikola's one-time publicist, now publicly supported Marconi. Investors on Wall Street began to back Marconi's work and called Wardenclyffe Tower a hoax. Nikola ignored the bad press that he began to receive and turned to his patron, John Pierpont Morgan, for additional funds. In July 1903, he wrote to Morgan and explained his situation. "Financially, I am in a dreadful fix," he said. Yet, he still made claims of being able to deliver a "World Telegraphy System." By this time, however, Morgan had lost faith in Wardenclyffe Tower. He felt that Nikola had failed to deliver on his promises and refused to provide him with any more money.

Without Morgan's support, Nikola was forced to abandon Wardenclyffe Tower in the late summer of

Nikola refused to give up on his vision of the wireless transmission of energy.

1905. Twelve years later, the tower was demolished. Yet, Nikola refused to give up on his vision of the wireless transmission of energy. After suffering another nervous breakdown, he returned to New York City and took up residence in the Waldorf-Astoria hotel. Once again with no means to support himself, Nikola lived there for the next several years on credit. It was a difficult time. The loss of several close friends and associates over the next decade made life even harder to bear. By 1914, William Rankine, Stanford White, Mark Twain, John Jacob Astor, and George Westinghouse had all died. Fighting depression, Nikola once again turned to electrotherapy to cope. At the same time, he struggled to think of another invention that would save his failing career.

Later Years

Nikola never gave up on his ideas about the transmission of power through wireless means. However, his failure to get these ideas to work on a practical level left him feeling frustrated. After recovering from a nervous breakdown in 1906, Nikola turned his attention from electricity to mechanical engineering. He collected enough money to rent a small office in the Singer Sewing Machine Building in lower Manhattan and went back to work. He found inspiration in a recent event that had taken place near Kitty Hawk, North Carolina. In 1903, Orville and Wilbur Wright had invented and flown the world's first successful airplane, ushering in a new age of human-powered flight. This reminded Nikola of his childhood dream of creating a flying machine. He began to read everything he could about the Wright brothers' break-through. Before long, he came up with a new idea.

Nikola learned that the Wright brothers had used a lightweight, gasoline-powered engine to get their airplane into the air. However, he was certain he could improve on their design. With the help of Julius Czito, the son of a former assistant from his Colorado Springs laboratory, Nikola produced the model of a bladeless turbine engine in July 1906. The model weighed less than 50 pounds and was able to deliver 110 horsepower. It came to be known as the Tesla turbine. Nikola was never able to turn his invention into a practical device, but he attracted the attention of Waltham Watch Company of Waltham, Massachusetts. The firm saw the potential that Nikola's research could have on precision instruments and offered to do business with him. This led to the development of Nikola's speed indicator. Once again, however, Nikola's lack of business sense allowed the Waltham Watch Company to secure the patent for itself instead of for its inventor.

When World War I—the Central Powers (Austria-Hungary and Germany) against the Allies (France, Russia, the United Kingdom, and, eventually, the United States)—began in 1914, the British navy immediately severed the undersea transatlantic cables that connected Germany with the rest of the world. However, the radio stations in New York and New Jersey kept Germany in contact with the United States, which was a neutral country at the beginning of the war. But the British government was determined to stop the flow of information between Germany and America. The British government asked the Marconi Wireless Telegraph Company to sue the Atlantic Communication Company and the German corporation Telefunken for patent infringement. When the case went to court, Telefunken sent two physicists—Jonathan Zenneck and Karl Ferdinand Braun—as part of their defense team. They also hired Nikola as a witness, paying him $1,000 a month over a period of two years. These developments made Nikola decide to sue Marconi in August 1915 for infringing upon his wireless patent design. Both lawsuits continued until 1917 when the cases were dropped. In April of that year, the United States finally declared war on Germany. At that point, communication between the two countries was no longer a legal issue.

Like many Americans after the United States entered the war, Nikola wanted to help the U.S. government in any way he could. By this time, he was a committed *pacifist*, that is, a person strongly opposed to war. Inspired by his beliefs, Nikola focused his mind on an idea that he hoped would bring the conflict to a speedy conclusion. Waging an aggressive war against the Allies, Germany used its fleet of U-boats (submarines) to great effect. Yet Nikola was certain he could find a way to detect them. His proposed concept of using an electric wave to locate the submarines' metal hulls beneath the waves faced many difficulties. When the war ended in 1918, Nikola's ideas were still on the drawing board. A generation later, however, the military had developed this concept, which is known today as radar, and used it to its full potential during World War II (1939-1945).

On Nov. 6, 1915, Nikola received some news that filled him with joy. Reuters, an international news agency based in London, reported that he and Thomas Edison had won the Nobel Prize in physics. Nikola, who had not received official notice of this great honor, told the press that he believed the honor had been given to him for his groundbreaking work in the wireless transmission of electrical energy. Nine days later, however, the Royal Swedish Academy of Sciences announced that the report was false. Neither Nikola nor Edison had received the Nobel Prize. Instead, it was given to the British physicists William Henry Bragg (1862-1942) and his son, William Lawrence Bragg (1890-1971), for their work in the study of X rays. Nikola was angry and embarrassed by Reuter's highly publicized mistake. The following year, Nikola was summoned to appear in court by the city of New York for failing to pay $935 in taxes. Nikola explained to the court that he was living on credit at the Waldorf-Astoria and unable to pay his bills. On the official record, he was forced to reveal that his company had no real assets and that he received only a small amount in royalties to cover his basic expenses. Nikola never really recovered from this public humiliation.

In the years that followed World War I, Nikola became more and more withdrawn from society. In

Nikola was featured on the cover of *Time* magazine on July 20, 1931, in honor of his 75th birthday. For the next few years, reporters flocked to his New York City hotel room to mark his birthday.

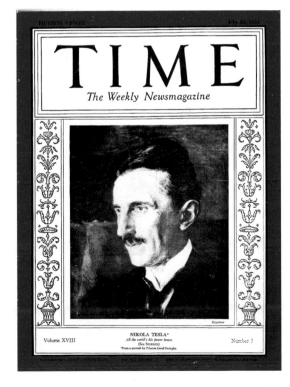

FIFTEEN CENTS

July 20, 1931

TIME
The Weekly Newsmagazine

NIKOLA TESLA*
All the world's his power house.
(See SCIENCE)
From a portrait by Princess Lwoff-Parlaghy.

Volume XVIII

Number 3

1922, he moved to the St. Regis hotel, leaving behind a large, unpaid bill at the Waldorf-Astoria. When Katharine Johnson, one of his few surviving friends, died in 1925, Nikola's isolation only increased. His behavior became more and more eccentric. Never having married, he now seemed to find his only companionship with the pigeons he found near his hotel. He was often seen feeding them near St. Patrick's Cathedral and the New York Public Library, two landmarks along famous Fifth Avenue in Manhattan. Apparently, Nikola even brought some of the pigeons back to his hotel room. He was particularly fond of one of them. "As long as I had her," Nikola said, "there was purpose in my life." When the bird died, he was brokenhearted. Nikola's care for the city's pigeons was a source of annoyance for staff at the St. Regis hotel. Noticing an unpleasant smell coming from Nikola's room and a large amount of pigeon droppings on the windowsills outside, the hotel management evicted him. For the rest of his life, Nikola was forced to move from hotel to hotel every few years, leaving his bills unpaid.

In 1931, a young science writer named Kenneth Swezey organized a celebration in honor of Nikola's 75th birthday. Through Swezey's efforts, Nikola was featured on the cover of *Time* magazine. For the next several years, the press flocked to Nikola's hotel every year to mark his birthday. Nikola was only too happy to be interviewed by the journalists and made surprising claims about his work. In 1932, he told a gathering of reporters that he had invented a motor that would run on "cosmic rays." Two years later, he said he had created a new super weapon. Referring to it as a "death ray," he predicted it would bring an end to war once and for all. However, proof of these inventions never came to light.

One evening in August 1937, Nikola left his room at the New Yorker Hotel to feed his beloved pigeons. As he crossed the street, he was struck by a taxicab. Nikola's back was severely injured and three of his ribs were broken. With his lifelong fear of doctors, Nikola refused to have his injury treated and limped back to his hotel. His health declined over the next several years.

On Jan. 7, 1943, at the age of 86, Nikola Tesla died quietly in his sleep. One of the hotel maids, ignoring the "do not disturb" sign hanging on the door, entered his room and found his body. Mysteriously, agents of the U.S. Federal Bureau of Investigation raided his room two days later and seized Nikola's belongings. At the time, many suspected the government was in search of designs for the "death ray" that Nikola claimed to have invented. On January 12, more than 2,000 mourners attended Nikola's funeral at the Episcopal Cathedral of St. John the Divine in Manhattan. The mayor of New York, Fiorello La Guardia, gave the eulogy. Afterward, Nikola's body was taken to the cemetery in Ardsley, New York. There, in a private ceremony, his body was cremated.

In the last years of his life, Nikola's only companions seemed to be the pigeons he found near his hotel. He was particularly fond of a white female pigeon, similar to the one pictured above, and was brokenhearted when the bird died.

Legacy

Nikola Tesla was undeniably a genius, a visionary, and a man ahead of his times. Since his death in 1943, people have greatly benefited from his inventions. Honored for his many achievements as a young man, Tesla was all but forgotten toward the end of his life. Only recently has the world once again taken notice of him. Joining the ranks of such inventors as Thomas Edison and Guglielmo Marconi, Nikola Tesla now stands perhaps even taller than these two great men. Yet, the story of his life cannot be told without recalling his unrealized potential. Although he registered hundreds of patents during his lifetime, Nikola left behind few blueprints that could have illuminated the way for some of the great minds that came after him.

With his ideas about the wireless transmission of power, Tesla saw himself as a revolutionary. He expected his technological innovations to make the existing systems of communication—the telegraph and the telephone—things of the past. Yet, again and again, he failed to raise the necessary funds for his research and lost the trust of such men as John Pierpont Morgan. Consequently, many of his greatest ideas remained unfulfilled. Tesla himself said that imagination—conceiving an idea that will change the world—was only the beginning of an inventor's work. The spark of a brilliant idea must always be followed by long hours spent in developing one's ideas and supported by the ability to communicate this vision to others. This, more than anything else, remains Nikola Tesla's enduring legacy and greatest lesson for the inventors of tomorrow.

INDEX

FURTHER READING

Aldrich, Lisa J. *Nikola Tesla and the Taming of Electricity.* Morgan Reynolds, 2005.

Carlson, W. Bernard. *Tesla: Inventor of the Electrical Age.* Princeton, 2013.

Cooper, Christopher. *The Truth About Tesla: The Myth of the Lone Genius in the History of Innovation.* Race Point, 2015.

Yount, Lisa. *Nikola Tesla: Harnessing Electricity.* Chelsea Hse., 2012.

ACKNOWLEDGMENTS

Cover: © ullstein bild/Getty Images

3-15 Public Domain

16 © Nikola Tesla Museum/Science Photo Library

19 © Imagno/Getty Images

20 © Hein Nouwens, Shutterstock

23-31 Public Domain

33 © Chris Hunter, Getty Images

36 United States Patent and Trademark Office

41 © SSPL/Getty Images

42 Public Domain

45 © Nikola Tesla Museum/Science Photo Library

49-51 Public Domain

53 © Nikola Tesla Museum/Science Photo Library

58-62 Public Domain

66-69 © Nikola Tesla Museum/Science Photo Library

70 Public Domain

73 © Getty Images

75-76 Public Domain

79 © Nikola Tesla Museum/Science Photo Library

80 © Getty Images

83 © FPG/Archive Photos/Getty Images

89 Public Domain

91 © Nikola Tesla Museum/Science Photo Library